SUPER SANDCASTLE™

Animal Habitats

What Lives in the Savanna?

Oona Gaarder-Juntti

Consulting Editor, Diane Craig, M.A./Reading Specialist

ABDO
Publishing Company

Published by ABDO Publishing Company, 8000 West 78th Street, Edina, Minnesota 55439. Copyright © 2009 by Abdo Consulting Group, Inc. International copyrights reserved in all countries. No part of this book may be reproduced in any form without written permission from the publisher. Super SandCastle™ is a trademark and logo of ABDO Publishing Company.

Printed in the United States.

Credits
Editor: Liz Salzmann
Content Developer: Nancy Tuminelly
Cover and Interior Design and Production: Oona Gaarder-Juntti, Mighty Media
Illustration: Oona Gaarder-Juntti
Photo Credits: Photodisc, ShutterStock

Library of Congress Cataloging-in-Publication Data

Gaarder-Juntti, Oona, 1979-

What lives in the savanna? / Oona Gaarder-Juntti.

p. cm. -- (Animal habitats)

ISBN 978-1-60453-178-7

1. Savanna animals--Juvenile literature. I. Title.

QL115.3G33 2009

591.7'48--dc22

2008005480

Super SandCastle™ books are created by a team of professional educators, reading specialists, and content developers around five essential components—phonemic awareness, phonics, vocabulary, text comprehension, and fluency—to assist young readers as they develop reading skills and strategies and increase their general knowledge. All books are written, reviewed, and leveled for guided reading, early reading intervention, and Accelerated Reader® programs for use in shared, guided, and independent reading and writing activities to support a balanced approach to literacy instruction.

About SUPER SANDCASTLE™

Bigger Books for Emerging Readers
Grades K–4

Created for library, classroom, and at-home use, Super SandCastle™ books support and engage young readers as they develop and build literacy skills and will increase their general knowledge about the world around them. Super SandCastle™ books are part of SandCastle™, the leading PreK–3 imprint for emerging and beginning readers. Super SandCastle™ features a larger trim size for more reading fun.

Let Us Know
Super SandCastle™ would like to hear your stories about reading this book. What was your favorite page? Was there something hard that you needed help with? Share the ups and downs of learning to read. We want to hear from you! Send us an e-mail.

sandcastle@abdopublishing.com

Contact us for a complete list of SandCastle™, Super SandCastle™, and other nonfiction and fiction titles from ABDO Publishing Company.

www.abdopublishing.com • 8000 West 78th Street Edina, MN 55439 • 800-800-1312 • 952-831-1632 fax

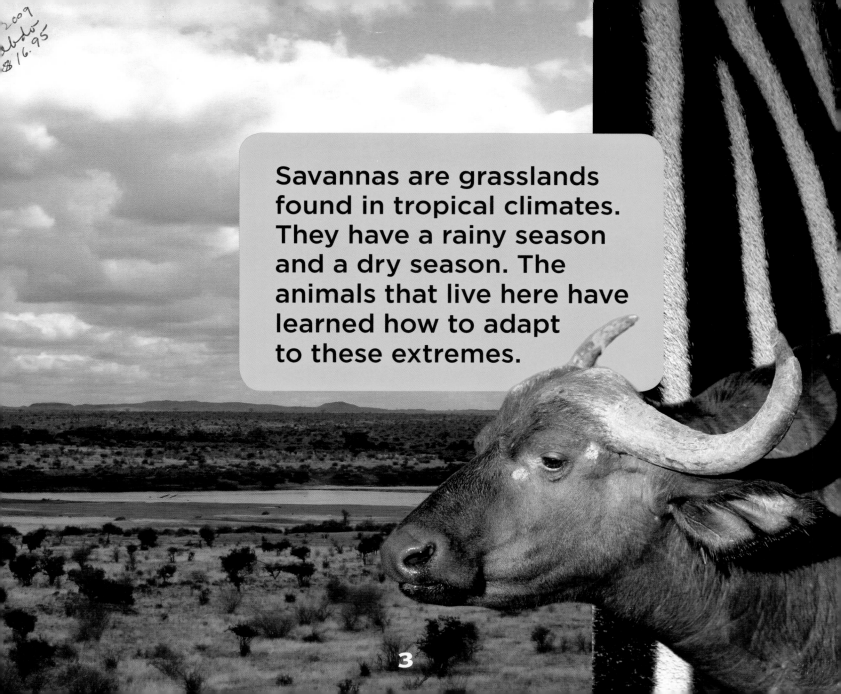

Savannas are grasslands
found in tropical climates.
They have a rainy season
and a dry season. The
animals that live here have
learned how to adapt
to these extremes.

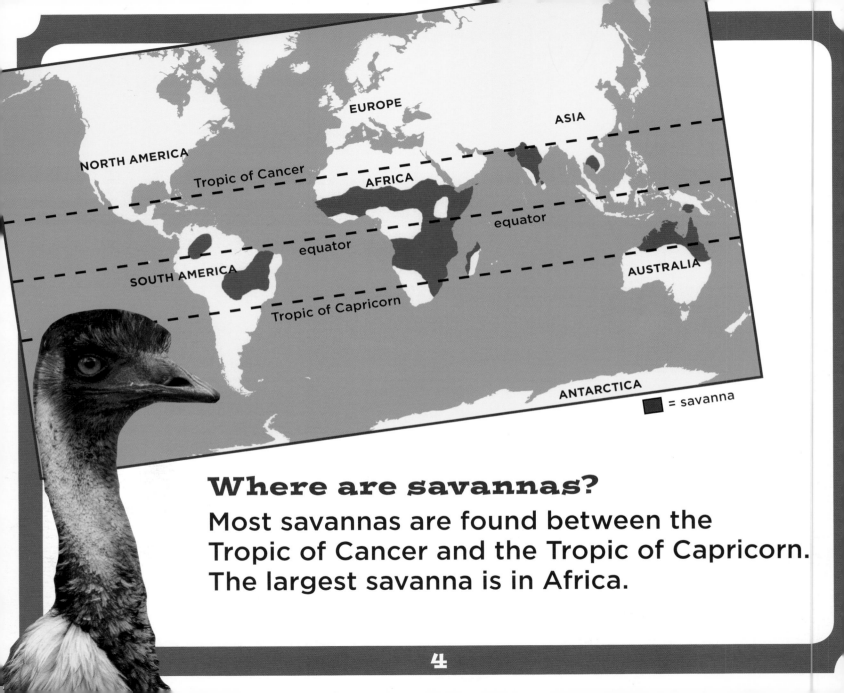

EUROPE

ASIA

NORTH AMERICA

Tropic of Cancer

AFRICA

equator

SOUTH AMERICA

equator

AUSTRALIA

Tropic of Capricorn

ANTARCTICA

= savanna

Where are savannas?

Most savannas are found between the Tropic of Cancer and the Tropic of Capricorn. The largest savanna is in Africa.

What does the savanna look like?

The savanna is flat with long grasses and very few trees.

KANGAROO

Animal class: Mammal
Location: Australia

Kangaroos are the largest marsupials in the world. They have powerful back legs. They can hop faster than 30 miles per hour.

A baby kangaroo is called a joey. The joey will stay in its mother's pouch for seven to nine months.

LION

Animal class: Mammal
Location: Africa

Lions live in groups called prides. Female lions do most of the hunting for the pride. They hunt together at night.

Male lions have thick manes that help protect their necks during fights.

OSTRICH

Animal class: Bird
Location: Africa

Ostriches are the largest and heaviest birds. They are too big to fly. They can run faster than 40 miles per hour.

Ostriches have the largest eyes of any land animal. Their eyes are two inches wide.

ZEBRA

Animal class: Mammal
Location: Africa

Zebras have stripes to protect them from predators. It is hard for predators to pick one zebra out of a herd. Every zebra has a different pattern of stripes.

Zebras show their teeth as a friendly greeting to other zebras.

GIRAFFE

Animal class: Mammal
Location: Africa

Giraffes are the tallest of all land animals. They can be up to 18 feet tall! Their height helps them reach leaves on tall trees.

Giraffes have blue-black tongues that are 18 inches long.

HIPPOPOTAMUS

Animal class: Mammal
Location: Africa

Hippos stay cool by spending the day in water or mud. They move through lakes and rivers by walking on the bottom. They can hold their breath for up to five minutes.

Hippos use their long teeth for fighting and defending themselves.

RHINOCEROS

Animal class: Mammal
Location: Africa and Asia

Some species of rhinos have one horn. Other species have two horns. Rhinoceros means "nose horn" in Greek. Rhinos can't see very well.

Oxpeckers ride on rhinos. They eat ticks that live on the rhinos. They also warn the rhino of approaching danger.

AFRICAN ELEPHANT

Animal class: Mammal
Location: Africa

African elephants are the world's heaviest land mammals. They use their trunks for breathing, communicating, smelling, and picking things up.

Elephants drink by sucking water into their trunks and pouring it into their mouths.

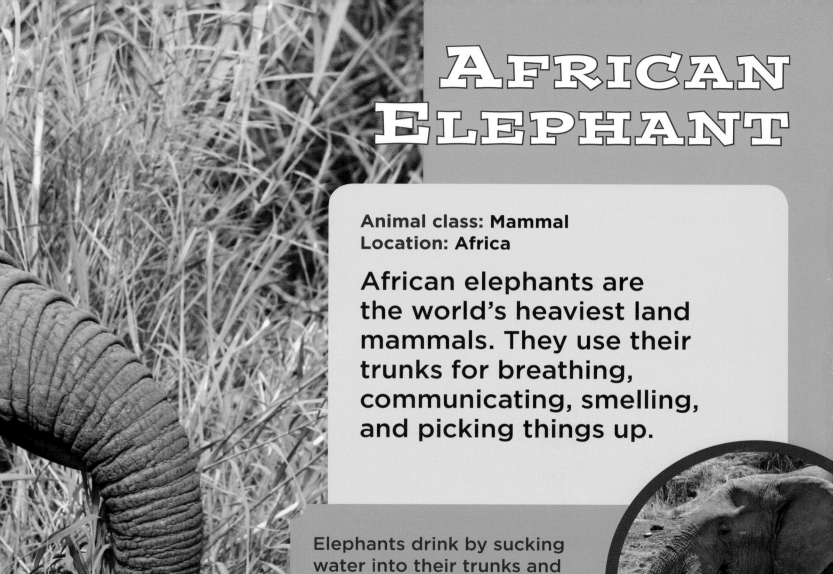

Have you ever been to a savanna?

More Savanna Animals

Can you learn about these savanna animals?

aardvark	giant anteater
antelope	hyena
augur buzzard	impala
baboon	jaguar
black mamba	leopard
blue wildebeest	llama
cape buffalo	mongoose
capybara	Nile crocodile
cheetah	wallaby
emu	wombat

GLOSSARY

adapt – to change in order to function better for a specific need or situation.

climate – the usual weather in a place.

communicate – to share ideas, information, or feelings.

defend – to protect from harm or attack.

extreme – either end of a range.

female – being of the sex that can produce eggs or give birth. Mothers are female.

height – how tall something is.

male – being of the sex that can father offspring. Fathers are male.

mammal – a warm-blooded animal that has hair and whose females produce milk to feed the young.

marsupial – a mammal in which the female has a pouch in which the young develop.

pouch – a pocket-like space on the belly in which marsupials carry their young.

predator – an animal that hunts others.

protect – to guard someone or something from harm or danger.

tropical – located in the hottest areas on earth.

trunk – an elephant's upper lip and long nose.